The Western Front 1914—1918

D. R. BANTING

and

G. A. EMBLETON

ALMARK PUBLISHING CO. LTD.
LONDON

First published 1974

ISBN 0 85524 172 I (hard cover edition)

ISBN 0 85524 173 X (paper covered edition)

Printed in Great Britain by
Chapel River Press, Andover, Hants SP10 3NS,
for the publishers, Almark Publishing Co Ltd,
49 Malden Way, New Malden,
Surrey KT3 6EA, England.

Introduction...

THE WAR TO END ALL WARS

A STUDY of World War 1 may be approached from several different sides, from the nations involved in it to the people themselves, for example. It may be viewed as a succession of thrilling incidents, or as often futile attempts to achieve vague objectives, or as an episode in the continuing history of Europe, as a watershed between the stability of the Victorian Age and the restlessness of the 20th Century, or as yet another example of man's inhumanity to man.

The limited space afforded by this slim volume has necessitated a basically factual account. It is an introduction to a very complex subject, and it is hoped that sufficient interest may be aroused for the reader to delve deeper into more lengthy works.

On November 11, 1918, a machine-gun section somewhere on the Western Front received this message:

'Hostilities will cease at 11 am today. Form up and march back independently to the Chateau Harveng, at once. Do not forget to bring the cookers with you.'

An armistice had been signed and had brought to an end a war which had cost the world nine million lives. Forgive maybe, but we should never forget that in a little over four years 1,000,000 men of the British forces by land, sea and air had died. The German dead numbered nearer 2,000,000, the Russians even more; France had almost 1,400,000 killed; Austria 1,200,000; Italy 460,000; Turkey 300,000 and the United States of America 116,000. Remember also that these figures do not include the merchant seamen who perished, the civilian victims of bombardments and air raids, or the Armenians who died by the thousand while being deported by the Turks. Nor is allowance made for the millions of men hopelessly crippled, tragically blinded or rendered insane.

It all happened over fifty years ago. It is history like the Romans, William the Conqueror or Trafalgar. But is it? The 'Great' War was such a big eruption in the history of Europe that it set up tremors the vibrations of which we still feel today. The memory of the war is ineradicably part of our lives. A few old but still proud 'contemptibles' are still in evidence on each anniversary of the signing of the armistice. The silence of the battlefields on that first armistice day is imagined by those too young to remember, and those with respect and feeling stand in silent tribute to those who fell. Life today might be very different if they had not made their sacrifice. The passing of the years may have diminished some of the early poignancy, but we owe too much to those men and women to shrug them off as a piece of ancient history. Remembrance poppies are still bought and sold even if their sale has to be justified to an increasing number of innocents every year.

Our hospitals still contain victims of the war who have been bed-ridden for fifty years. Men who have given youth, limbs, faculties or senses and who have lain helplessly ever since as a reward.

It can be argued that the British national economy is still feeling the effects of World War 1 today. After 1918 never again would Britannia be sole commander of the seas and governess of the maritime trading routes. The commercial ties of Empire were beginning to fray. The Dominions were asserting their independence. Prices which went up at the time seldom came down again. The direct costs of the conflict are still being met today with the payments rightly being made to dependants of those who played their part in the war, and for the treatment and assistance of those unable to fend for themselves since 1918.

The civilians of countries not actually in the front line were seriously affected for the first time. The horror and the cost of total war was brought home literally, to the whole nation. All were involved in the war effort, young and old, servicemen and shopkeepers, factory workers and farmers.

Women did their bit as well. They worked in the factories or on the farms or took over the jobs of men called to the war, and by their efforts kept the wheels of industry turning and won the right to vote for their representatives in the British Parliament. They finally won full emancipation several years later after hostilities had ended, but female agitation has proved to be an organic process currently re-emerging in the Women's Liberation Movement.

So many died in the Great War that most families lost a father, a brother, a son, a friend or neighbour. It was an age when commanders could take men to their death in the name of nothing but honour. Just look at the lists of names on your local memorial. This is hardly surprising when it is realised that horrors like aerial bombing, gas attacks and tank warfare, which seem to hold a permanent place in today's television, were first introduced and developed in the years between 1914 and 1918.

Holiday-makers in Turkey today are offered souvenirs of the ill-fated Gallipoli landings. Rusty weapons and even human bones are gleaned from the peninsula's shores by local beachcombers with an eye for the tourist market.

On a more happy note, various forms of entertainment constantly remind us of those momentous years. Songs like 'Tipperary', first launched by Florrie Ford in 1913, and 'Pack up your troubles in your old kit bag' which first found favour on the roads and in the trenches of northern France are still sung with an air of comradeship on group outings today. The evergreen popularity of war films, traditionally heroic, but more recently also, as the fervour of nationalism and patriotism dies down, of the 'de-bunking' type, constantly remind us of both the glory and the futility of the war. 'All quiet on the Western Front', 'King and Country' and 'Oh what a lovely war' spring readily to mind. For those a little younger, comics for boys often seem to include at least one soldier hero along with the brilliant spaceman and the miraculous sportsman. The prose and verse of Robert Graves and the poetry of Edmund Blunden, Rupert Brooke and Wilfred Owen retain their popularity as today's readers come to understand the deep feelings which experience inspired in these and other writers of that tragic period.

4

THE SPREADING FLAME

In June 1914 the heir to the Austrian throne, Franz Ferdinand, paid a State visit to Bosnia, a country annexed against its will. In addition, the day chosen, June 28th, was Saint Vitus's day, a Serbian holiday when national feelings might be expected to run high. The local security forces of Sarajevo had warned the Archduke of the difficulty of giving him adequate protection, and even as he was leaving the railway station an attempt was made on his life. Later, as his procession was driving through the town, a Serbian conspirator, Gavrilo Princip, ran from the crowd and shot dead both Franz Ferdinand and his wife.

Austria consequently demanded that Serbia should become part of the Austro-Hungarian Empire, but Russia, the champion of the slavonic cause, advised Serbia not to submit. Austria accordingly declared war on Serbia; Russia mobilised to protect her. Germany, because of the terms of her Triple Alliance with Austria, declared war on Russia, and because France mobilised to help Russia, under the terms of the Triple Entente, (between France, Russia and Britain), Germany then declared war on France. German forces marched through Belgium which Britain had promised to support so Britain then declared war on Germany. 'The war to end all wars' had begun.

What happened to Gavrilo Princip?

He was born a peasant in the Bosnian village Oblej on July 13, 1894. Nineteen years later, at point-blank range, he fired two shots from a Browning revolver. The first struck the Archduke Franz Ferdinand in his jugular vein. The second hit his Duchess in the stomach. Both were dead within the hour.

By August 4, as the Germans marched into Belgium, Princip was undergoing daily interrogation. With fellow conspirators he was tried and sentenced in October. As he was a minor he escaped capital punishment, but he died of consumption in the fortress of Theresienstadt before the war which he had precipitated had ended.

Declarations of War, 1914-1918

July 28, 1914	Austria-Hungary on Serbia
August 1, 1914	Germany on Russia
August 3, 1914	Germany on France
August 4, 1914	Great Britain on Germany
August 4, 1914	Germany on Belgium
August 5, 1914	Montenegro on Austria-Hungary
August 12, 1914	Great Britain on Austria-Hungary
November 2, 1914	Russia on Turkey
November 6, 1914	Britain and France on Turkey
May 23, 1915	Italy on Austria-Hungary
October 6, 1915	Bulgaria and Serbia on each other
October 15, 1915	Britain on Bulgaria
October 16, 1915	France on Bulgaria
October 19, 1915	Italy and Russia on Bulgaria
March 9, 1916	Germany on Portugal
August 27, 1916	Rumania on Austria-Hungary
April 6, 1917	United States of America on Germany
July 12, 1918	Haiti on Germany
July 31, 1918	Onodaga Indian nation on Germany

A German cemetery. There are over a million bodies in military cemeteries in different parts of the world—a fraction of the total dead of the Great War, since many had no burial at all (Imperial War Museum).

Four of the two million Frenchmen killed or maimed in just over four years (Imperial War Museum).

Refitted at Government expense: A German (above), a Frenchman (below). Occupations perhaps indicative of national character (Imperial War Museum).

The Great Powers in 1914

BRITAIN

FRANZ Ferdinand was killed in Sarajevo on June 28, 1914 but it was not until July 21st that *The Times* developed the story on its front page. In fourteen days Britain would be at war, but her people remained preoccupied with their daily round of work, holidays (the weather was glorious that summer), and sport. Sport, indeed, had become almost an obsession. Cricket, soccer, (Burnley were currently holders of the Football Association Challenge Cup), All-England Tennis contests and rowing, (America had just carried off their first major prize at Henley), reigned supreme in the minds of Britain's millions.

Still reading, perhaps of their Majesties' recent visit to Scotland, attending cinema shows which were just then beginning to boast a vast improvement with sensational drama and rollicking comedies, bewailing the fact that gin was six pence (2½p) a double and cigarettes five pence half-penny (almost 2½p) for twenty—these were of more importance than any potential showdown with Germany. Anyway, were not George V, the Kaiser and the Czar all related and friends together?

But although the warnings of Lord Roberts had largely gone unheard, Britain was not entirely unprepared for war. She was the world's leading naval power and her great Empire, greater than that of Rome, greater than that of the Mongols, was kept close to the Motherland by the Royal Navy. In the fateful summer of 1914 two hundred and sixty vessels of the British Fleet were drawn up at Spithead for an inspection by George V. They were destined not to disperse but to pass straight to their battle stations.

On land the War Office had recently been reorganised, a General Staff created, an expeditionary force set up and a second line Territorial Army established. It is also worth noting that, of all the major European armies only Britain's had experience of recent action, and in the Short Magazine Lee Enfield rifle the British soldier had the most comfortable and accurate firearm in the world.

A third example of Britain's preparedness was Lord Hankey's famous War Book, completed on July 14, 1914, and which laid down in precise details procedures to be adopted by every department of public life in the event of a major war.

Prime Minister Asquith, however, was reluctant to commit the nation to a war which, despite popular feeling at the time, just might possibly last for a long time. But Germany broke her promise not to invade Belgium and on August 4th Britain declared war on Germany. The Aldershot Command received a telegram which simply said 'Mobilise Troopers'. Churchill had already deployed the fleet against surprise attack. Crowds gathered outside Buckingham Palace and sang 'God save the King' with patriotic gusto. The tension had been released. 'Now let us get on with the job of defeating the Kaiser' was the common feeling, and there was to be no shortage of volunteers to fight the wicked Hun. In fact, the magnificent response to Kitchener's appeal for troops is one of the great events of British history. 'Defeat Germany for the sake of peace and disarmament throughout the world', said H. G. Wells. There was a widespread relief that became almost a rapture, and the confidence of it all—'Berlin by Christmas'. Some, however, still failed to recognise the significance of the Government's declaration. A vicar's wife, for example, wrote, 'the maid woke me to give me a delayed telegram. It was from S, then a naval cadet, saying he had been ordered abroad and would need money. I hurried to the Post Office to telegraph some to him . . . There was little time to think of war . . . because a huge charity fete was taking place'.

On August 4, 1914 Britain declared war on Germany, and without first consulting her Dominions or colonies overseas. This was an example of extreme faith and confidence for without their manpower and economic support defeat would have been a strong probability. Her other 'Allies' were to be France, Russia, Belgium, Serbia, Japan, Italy (after 1915), Portugal and Rumania (after 1916), and the United States of America (after 1917).

The enemy were the 'Central Powers' of Germany, Austria, Turkey and Bulgaria.

This division of Europe had come about largely as a result of the 1882 'Triple Alliance' between Germany, Austria and originally Italy, and the 'Triple Entente' dating from 1894 between Britain, France and Russia.

GERMANY

Of all the countries involved in the Great War, Germany was the most prepared. Not surprising, as she was the aggressor, but remember that it was Britain who declared war on Germany, not the reverse. Since the Franco-Prussian war of 1870-71 Germany had been afraid that France might seek revenge, and had, therefore, kept her military forces and equipment in perfect readiness for the showdown when it came. She had made alliances with Austria and Italy to secure a friendly bloc of countries in central Europe. The German naval building programme was accelerated to rival Britain's mastery of the seas and to assist Kaiser Wilhelm's colonial policy. Germany and the German people had been preparing for an inevitable war.

Frankfurt, in early August, 1914, and Walter Bloem, a Captain in the 12th Brandenburg Grenadiers, like many others was making his last minute personal arrangements. He went shopping and purchased field boots, torches and a pair of binoculars, then made the rounds saying goodbye to his friends and neighbours.

When war broke out Germany could have thrown about two and a half million men into the field. This gave them a numerical advantage over either the British or the French armies, and as the Russians were both badly led and poorly armed, the German army presented the most formidable fighting machine in Europe. One of the reasons for their early casualties being so high was that they tended to move in heavy, close formations and to attack in solid masses. This undid the advantage which their field grey uniforms initially gave them over the more conspicuous colourings of the French.

Stories and rumours about the enemy were rife in the Allied trenches. Atrocities, which must have taken place, were exaggerated, and truth, as usual, was an early casualty in the war. Germany was probably the first to deliberately attempt to mislead her public, when, on August 3rd, some of her newspapers announced the bombing of railway lines between Karlsruhe and Nuremburg by the French. Another mythical report described an attempt by Frenchmen dressed in Prussian uniforms trying to cross the frontier at Waldeck. Despite French reports to the contrary the Prussian Guards were not all giants, although in fairness to the instigators of this tale, the bodies of several seven-foot guardsmen were found after the first Battle of Ypres. A less sinister story is told of a notice board erected in front of a German trench and facing the British which read 'we are Saxons, you are Anglo-Saxons. Do not fire and we will not'.

All the armies of 1914 were composed of individual human beings. They all ate army rations and complained. They all hated the cold, the damp and the filth of the trenches. They all became tired. They all felt fear and wanted to stay alive. Yet in those early months of the tragedy a few voices only spoke in revulsion of the inevitable. One of the few was Albert Einstein who deplored 'this species which boasts of its freedom of will and yet makes war'.

FRANCE

As usual Paris in the early summer of 1914 was a show place for foreign visitors. The ladies were dutifully following the dictates of fashion and were wearing satins, silks and chiffon in the 'correct' colours of black and white, and their dresses were set off with large, shady hats. A new daring dance called the tango was all the rage and society talk was still of the recent visit by the King and Queen of England to the French capital. 'Gorgeous' Georges Carpentier was the boxing hero of the nation. Paris was then, as now, a centre of both culture and popular entertainment, a place for enjoyment and relaxation.

But psychologically France was not unprepared for war. On Saturday, August 8th, faced with a brutal German ultimatum, mobilisation notices appeared and the following Sunday saw almost every train in the country carrying reservists. Boulevard cafés played the 'Marseillaise' almost continuously. Foreign sympathisers offered their services to the French Government, and mobs destroyed any shops with a German name. What lay behind this excited desire to teach the Germans a lesson?

In the war of 1870-71 Prussia had defeated France and had gained control of the rich mineral resources of Alsace and Lorraine. This loss of territory kindled a spirit of revenge in the hearts of the French. The flame was to flicker and die down but it had not been extinguished by 1914. Secondly, it may be a myth, but the fiery, Latin temperament supposedly characteristic of the French has been associated in the eyes of their critics with an insatiable thirst for glory through conquest or 'la Gloire'. The typical French soldier at the outbreak of hostilities was certainly brave, enthusiastic, maybe even over-zealous, active intelligent and adaptable, and he wanted revenge for his father's disgrace at Sedan.

Materially however, the French had problems in the early months of the war. A line of strong defences had been constructed along the hilly German frontier but these were to prove of little value, the initial German thrust being directed north of the line through the virtually unprotected Belgian Plain. On paper, German troops out-numbered those of France, so colonial forces had to be introduced and the length of military service extended to counteract the German superiority of numbers. In her 75 millimetre field-gun France possessed one of the most efficient weapons in the war, yet both her cavalry and infantry often suffered from being issued with weapons of a type originally designed for use forty years earlier. Hence the bayonet charges which were made against machine-guns. The French War Plan 17 itself was an ambitious gamble calling for a headlong assault against the German centre in the region of Lorraine. Heavy casualties were also suffered in the early engagements of the war before the French Command realised just how conspicuous their traditional red and blue uniforms made them.

AUSTRIA-HUNGARY

The Austro-Hungarian Empire in 1914 was a hotch-potch of cultures, religions and tongues. Germans, Croats, Czechs, Italians, Magyars, Serbs and Slovaks loosely held together under the throne of old Franz Joseph.

Austria was to be an ally of Germany but many authorities say that Germany was 'lumbered' with her. Indeed, it can be argued that it was Austria who was responsible for the holocaust that was to follow because of the totally unacceptable ultimatum which she presented to Serbia after the assassination of Franz Ferdinand, and by the way in which she left Germany no alternative but to support her in her aggression.

Serbia, as part of the Austrian Empire was, in 1914, the pivot of the Balkan situation. The Balkan countries had gained a measure of satisfaction from recent revolts against Turkish rule and this had served to further the Serbs' antagonism towards Austria-Hungary who had tended to support Turkey. June 28, 1914 dawned in Sarajevo, capital of the Austrian province of Bosnia, just as on any other summer's day, the muezzin called the faithful moslems to prayer, the market stall keepers set up their displays of fruit, vegetables, cheese and coffee, and the shabby peasants came down from the hills to pray and to buy. But before the day was out the spark that was to ignite Europe for the next four years had been fired by a young, unimportant student (whose name few remember today) at an unloved and unrespected Austrian prince.

RUSSIA

North and east of the Austrian Empire lay the sprawling mass of backward, decadent Russia. A nation sick at all levels of her society, within and without, from the Royal family and its parasitic monk, the drunken, lecherous Rasputin, down to the starving, illiterate, barefoot peasantry. Yet this feudal kingdom was to provide the vast bulk of the Allies' outward strength. Slow, clumsy, poorly led and badly equipped, nevertheless the Russian 'steam-roller' of 114 infantry and 36 cavalry divisions was a force to be reckoned with. Of all the combatant nations, with 12,000,000 men to call upon, the Czar had at his disposal the largest army in the world.

BELGIUM

Belgium, an early victim of the war, was in 1914 less than seventy-five years old, having been created by the welding together of Protestant Flemish speakers from the Dutch borders and the French speaking Walloons of the south. But her determined, if futile, attempts to defend her neutrality gave the war its first hero in the person of General Gerard Leman, commander of the garrison of Liège. Liège, at the outbreak of the war, consisted of a fortified region protected by twelve concrete and steel forts situated on both banks of the River Meuse. Some of the forts were as much as three miles apart and it therefore needed a whole field division of the Belgian army to plug the gaps between them. For several priceless days in August, 1914 the forts and Belgian infantry held the German advance but with terrible casualties on both sides. The defence of Liège was thereby Belgium's first contribution to the Allied cause.

SWITZERLAND

Switzerland's position at the hub of Europe was not without its dangers. Four of her neighbours overshadowed her in size and resources. Yet the keynote of Switzerland remained her independence (so often a characteristic of mountain people), and she remained neutral throughout the war. Indeed, her neutrality had not been violated since 1815. Instead she was destined to become a symbol of security and stability. A sanctuary for escaped prisoners of war, or for those just opting out unofficially, and a refuge of large foreign deposits. She suffered no attacks from the belligerents and, at the end of hostilities, emerged intact in the midst of devastated countries. She was envied and harshly criticised for having kept out of the conflict. Some went as far as to accuse her of lack of solidarity in refusing to take sides.

After the war Swiss statesmen realised that the concept of neutrality which had prevailed in the past had lost its meaning in modern Europe. Abstention was no longer enough. To justify herself, Switzerland must become an active participant in any scheme designed to create and maintain international understanding. When the seeds of the League of Nations were being propagated it was Motta, the Swiss Foreign Secretary, who took the initiative and pleaded in favour of the admission of Germany. The Geneva Convention and the International Red Cross are a tribute to the Swiss statesmen of the inter-war years.

The Netherlands and Scandinavian countries likewise managed to remain aloof. Indeed, it was to the former country that the German Kaiser escaped as his dreams shattered and his empire crumbled in the concluding weeks of 1918.

ITALY

Italy was even younger than Belgium. The Italian peninsula had become a united country only during the second half of the 19th Century. She was only just beginning to industrialise, and many of her people remained poor peasants. She had come too late into the race for empire, and her possessions overseas were of little importance. At the end of the last century Italy had been a member of the Triple Alliance with Germany and Austria, but in 1915 she was to enter the war on the side of the Allies.

TURKEY

Turkey was a declining power. In 1912 she had lost territory as a result of her defeat by Serbia, Bulgaria and Greece. She was a potential threat to Britain because of her proximity to the Suez Canal and Britannia's sea route to India and the Far East. There was also the old, old question of Russia casting covetous eyes on a routeway for her Black Sea fleet into the Mediterranean through Turkish waters.

THE UNITED STATES OF AMERICA

Removed from the main arenas of the war by the Atlantic Ocean, the United States was to make a late entry into the conflict. She regarded herself as the protector of the smaller nations of her continent, but did not wish to become involved in European quarrels. Instead she welcomed as immigrants the refugees from Europe's economic and political problems. In 1914 she did not even have a conscript army. Nevertheless she was to emerge from the war as the most powerful and highly industrialised nation in the world.

These were the powerful nations of 1914. They were stronger and richer than the rest of the world. They threatened each other and they made alliances with each other, but always protested that they did not want war. Nevertheless, all were determined to be on the right side should war break out, so insurance policies were taken out, armaments were stock-piled, soldiers trained and spy systems organised. Only the United States of America tried to remain aloof.

EUROPE 1914

Sir Edward Grey, the British Foreign Secretary in 1914. He strove hard to avert war. Britain's ultimatum to Germany expired at midnight on August 3; Grey was standing at a window of the Foreign Office watching the lamps being lit. He is said to have remarked: 'the lamps are going out all over Europe; we shall not see them lit again in our lifetime'.

Although undoubtedly an impulsive and volatile character, Kaiser Wilhelm II cannot be made to shoulder all the responsibility for the war. He was the sort of ruler that many Germans admired and he enjoyed widespread support throughout the German speaking world. He was aggressive and arrogant, typical of all the worst qualities of the adolescent and insecure German Empire.

King Albert of 'gallant little Belgium' (Imperial War Museum).

The War Lords. Field - Marshal Paul von Hindenburg, 1847 - 1934, and (below) General Erich Ludendorff, 1865-1937.

Victor Emmanuel III, King of Italy. He succeeded to the throne in 1900.

Nicholas II, Emperor of all the Russias, Supreme Commander - in - Chief of the world's greatest army in 1914.

Franz Joseph, Emperor of Austria.

One of the best stories of the Germany of Wilhelm II is the extraordinary but true tale of the Captain of Kopenick. One autumn day in 1906 a shoemaker, named Wilhelm Voigt, walked through Berlin dressed in the uniform of a captain in the German army. When he met four soldiers, he ordered them to fall in and to follow him. He was unknown to them but his uniform conferred such an air of authority upon his person that he was instantly obeyed. More troops were picked up and the party boarded a train for Kopenick, a small town just outside the German capital. Alighting at the suburb, Voigt set out for the town hall and on the way three policemen attached themselves to the uniformed band of marchers. Upon arriving at the town hall the 'Captain' successfully demanded that the sum of 4,002.50 Marks be paid to him. He signed a receipt and then ordered the arrest and removal from office of the mayor. Voigt's act lasted for about six hours before he too was arrested and returned to Berlin. He was later sentenced to four years' imprisonment. His story was in newspapers throughout Europe, and sympathetic letters and gifts poured into his prison. After two years he was released and, dressed in his now famous captain's uniform, he toured many European cities.

In her 75 mm field-gun France possessed one of the most efficient weapons in the war. Quick-firing and sturdy, it could be operated by a team of only three men (Imperial War Museum).

French Hussars seek guidance through mists in the Somme valley.

THE BRITISH ARMY

In 1914 the British Regular Army was the most modern fighting force in the world. Its standard of individual training was supreme. Apart from the Russian it was the only major European army to have seen recent action on a large scale. But its strength was only 11 infantry divisions —the same as Serbia—and three cavalry. True, they were Regulars and British volunteers, but few of their commanding officers had ever led more than a small group of men at one time. Even the Commander-in-Chief, Field Marshal Sir John French, who had distinguished himself in South Africa, was later criticised as being neither intellectually nor psychologically suited for the responsibilities thrust upon him.

During the course of the war, the British army passed through three distinct phases. Quite early in the exchanges the original Regulars had to be replaced by 'Kitchener's Volunteers' (he asked for 100,000 and within one year over 2,250,000 had offered their services), and then, as these in their turn were mown down, conscripted men took their places in the trenches.

At first, officers carried swords and wore uniforms of a distinctive cut showing their rank conspicuously in 'slashes' on their sleeves. But the reality of life at the Front soon saw them discarding such dress and turning to the private soldier's equipment with badges of rank worn less noticeably on their shoulder-straps. As informality crept in, only the Guards division continued to scrub their clothing, polish their leathers and drill amidst the mud of Northern France.

In 1902, following the South African War, khaki uniforms had become standard throughout the British army for all duties other than ceremonial. The British Expeditionary Force was consequently well equipped when the war broke out. The cap, which had been introduced in 1905, bore the regimental badge, and the shoulder-straps the name or initials in brass letters. In 1908 brown leather equipment for the men had been replaced with a woven material soon to be known throughout the world as 'webbing'. Puttees and boots completed the British soldier's uniform.

Probably the most significant change in the British uniforms during the war was the introduction, in 1915, of the steel helmet. As with other armies, life for the British in the frozen or flooded trenches led to the adoption of fur or leather jackets, scarves and mittens, gumboots, raincoats and waterproof headwear.

The Short Magazine Lee-Enfield No. 1 Mark III rifle had been introduced in 1907 and was the main infantry weapon used by the British throughout the war.

It is perhaps worth noting the basic equipment carried by the British infantryman. The average Tommy's 'fighting order' gear consisted of his normal clothing, including steel helmet and entrenching tool, but less the pack and greatcoat, plus:

ground sheet	two gas helmets
water-bottle	tear goggles
haversack	wire cutters
mess tin	field dressing
towel	iodine
shaving kit	220 rounds of ammunition
spare socks	two sand bags
message book	two Mills grenades
the unconsumed portion of the day's ration	

The total weight often exceeded 66 pounds, and then he was expected to run through the mud and over the wire, all the time under enemy fire —and fight.

17

YOUR
COUNTRY
NEEDS
YOU

The First World War saw graphic skill reach a high standard. Many posters illustrated national traits and appealed to a man's sense of duty and loyalty. Posters on hoardings, however, were a favourite target for cynical and ribald comments from the troops home on leave from the reality of life at the Front. The French bugler, as with many posters, emphasises nationalism and portrays a stirring call to arms in the spirit of La Gloire. The German example, with its concise and patriotic message of 'Help us to win—subscribe to the war loan', shows an infantryman as a hero of the Fatherland. When the United States entered the war in 1917 the bold, lush colouring of her posters exhibited the nation's youthful pride. The pointing finger motif, adopted so successfully in Britain, was copied and Lord Kitchener was replaced by Uncle Sam.

A daylight patrol of the 6th Seaforth Highlanders fire into apparently deserted German dug-outs to dislodge any of the enemy still lurking as snipers. The trench looks as if it has been abandoned for some time, and the scene may have been posed for the photographer. Note the khaki covers for the kilt with a pocket in place of a sporran (Imperial War Museum).

The Australians soon earned the reputation of being brave fighters and cheery allies, but also of being notoriously ill-disciplined troops. This photograph was taken near Amiens in September, 1916 (Imperial War Museum).

Worcesters hold the bank of Aisne at Maizy, May 27, 1918. The officer holds his service revolver at the ready (Imperial War Museum).

An officer in the Argyll and Sutherland Highlanders, 1919 (Imperial War Museum).

A rifleman in the Rifle Brigade, 1919 (Imperial War Museum).

A private in the 10th Argyll and Sutherland Highlanders, 1919. In the trenches the kilt was covered by a khaki apron (Imperial War Museum).

Left: Pioneer-Sturm-Bataillon (Nr. 5).

By 1918 most of the German Armies on the Western Front had a special Assault Battalion, each equipped with its own specialist teams and weapons (light artillery, machine guns, trench mortars and flame throwers). They were composed of strong, active and usually young troops, and were highly trained to spearhead attacks, and to carry out commando-style raids. They were so successful that by 1918 they had expanded into 18 battalions, each consisting of four assault companies, an Infantry artillery battery, a light trench mortar detachment, a flame-thrower detachment, a machine gun company and a Headquarters Company. The Assault troops were among the first to wear the steel helmet. This soldier is wearing the soft field-cap with the band and piping indicating his unit. He wears the same style jacket as worn in 1914. Most of the army had adopted a plain grey 'bluse' or fly-fronted jacket in the years 1915 to 1917. His knees are protected by leather patches and he wears puttees around his legs instead of boots. A short knife is carried for close quarter fighting and the bags slung at his sides contain grenades.

A 'Tommy' of 1916: He wears the greenish khaki issued throughout the British Army and is swathed with the usual canvas webbing equipment. His steel helmet is covered with a hessian cover. At first, a khaki, flat-topped Field Service cap was worn. During winter sheepskin and leather coats and jerkins were issued in large numbers. These were supplemented by countless unofficial additions and 'home comforts' like this man's mittens and Balaclava helmet. Puttees, long, khaki strips of cloth, were supposed to be wound around the calf nine times, finishing at the outer ankle bone. In practice, however, they were frequently wound in reverse, finishing at the knee. Blackened boots were the regulation issue.

THE FRENCH ARMY

Since the disasters of the Franco-Prussian War, France had built-up sixty-two infantry and ten cavalry divisions. Parts of the French Army machine were splendid: the adaptability and courage of the infantrymen, the resolution and ability of some of the commanders, and they had the famous 75 mm field gun. Nevertheless, mistakes were made, and thousands of Frenchmen died when they might have been better used and spared the supreme sacrifice. In 1914 the French army numbered some 1,250,000 men. By the end of the war her casualties exceeded 6,000,000.

The uniform of the French army underwent considerable changes in the course of the war, but at the outbreak of hostilities, despite various detail changes, the dress of the French infantryman remained much as it had been in 1870. The red képi had replaced the shako as parade headwear and was universally worn at the Front with grey or grey-blue covers. The blue tunic was simplified, during active service, with the abolition, in 1872, of the epaulettes and the introduction, at the turn of the century, of a single-breasted style. Otherwise trousers remained red and great coats were worn both winter and summer.

Even before the end of 1914, however, the French Command found it necessary to replace the conspicuous blue and red uniforms. The new colour was to be blue-grey (colonial troops wore khaki). It was probably chosen not only for its camouflage value but also because it was a contrast to the German field grey. Regimental numbers were shown on the collar patch. Officially, leather equipment was now to be brown, but black remained in use alongside the new colour for some considerable time. Puttees were introduced instead of leather leggings, and by 1915, the steel helmet, with its grenade decoration, was a more common sight than the képi.

Together with the Mannlicher-Berthier rifles, the 8 mm Lebel M1886/M1893 remained the French infantryman's personal weapon until well after the war was over. It was the first modern, mass-produced magazine rifle, and also introduced smokeless powder to the world.

The Front Line

barbed wire   breastwork with loopholes for rifle fire   firing step   sandbagged roof above dugout

General Silvestre and his staff in 1914. French dragoon officers' brass helmets, almost unchanged since Napoleonic times, are covered with cloth.

French troops in the Argonne district early in the war (Imperial War Museum).

The uniforms of 1914—the last time that the gay uniforms of the 18th and 19th centuries were to be seen on the battlefield. Developed to inspire 'esprit de corps' and patriotic enthusiasm they were useless in a war where weaponry ruled the field, and men needed to hide in the fields and mud. Left: A Belgian Infantryman 1914. Right: A French Infantryman 1914. Both campaign in their overcoats, the skirts hooked back to make marching easier.

Top left: French infantry Drummer in the red and blue traditional uniform of 1914. Top centre: Heroic representation of French Dragoon officer 1914. Top right: Little changed since Waterloo—the splendid uniform of French Cuirassiers in 1914. Above left: French infantryman in the uniform of 1914. Above right: Like the rest of the Army, the French Cavalry adopted horizon blue and steel helmets, like the British and German Cavalry they waited, usually in vain, for the big breakthrough. . . .

27

THE GERMAN ARMY

In the summer of 1914 the German army consisted of eighty-seven infantry and eleven cavalry divisions, a total of nearly 2,500,000 men.

Except for the famous spiked helmet and the fact that their officers still carried swords, their field-grey uniform was comparatively modern having been first issued in 1910. (Some of their peace-time full-dress uniforms, however, still retained traditional features such as the mitre-shaped grenadier cap, white trousers and the gorget or metallic neck-piece.) Leather equipment was blackened before troops left for the Front, cloth covers were worn over the helmet, buttons were oxidized and the polishing of metal items was suspended during time of war. German regulations also stated that the uniforms of officers should be more or less the same colour as those worn by the men.

In 1915 modifications were made to the 1910 field uniform. Trousers were now to be slate-grey and without trimmings. Puttees were more widely used when it was seen that the enemy favoured them and, more often than not, boots were blackened, as was the leather equipment. It was also found necessary to supply extra cartridge belts and these were worn either round the neck or over the shoulders. In 1916 a steel helmet began to replace the spiked, leather one and the infantry had to take to the gas mask.

The German infantryman was usually armed with either the 7.92 mm Mauser Gewehr 88 rifle (Germany's answer to France's 1886 Lebel), or the more sophisticated Mauser Gewehr 98, often called the world's most successful bolt-action rifle.

A Trench System

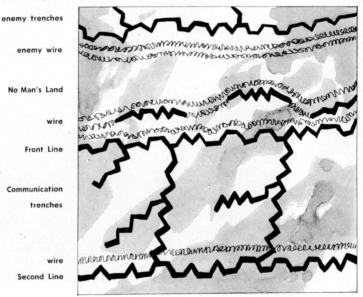

enemy trenches

enemy wire

No Man's Land

wire

Front Line

Communication

trenches

wire

Second Line

A trench system might consist of several lines of trenches, each with dugouts, barbed wire, etc, connected to each other by zig-zagging communication trenches. The Front Line was protected by masses of wire, and 'listening posts', and advance positions were made in no man's land.

Infantrymen captured at Messines Ridge June 8, 1917. The two helmeted soldiers in the front row wear the 1910 jacket—the other four wear the Bluse introduced in 1915-17. Note the soft field caps and puttees.

Infantrymen march to war. The officer wears the original field-grey uniform with the black and silver ribbon of the Iron Cross on his tunic front. The private's tunic has had the coloured cuff decorations removed (Imperial War Museum).

These officers wear the original regulation field-grey uniform tunic (Waffenrock) which was ordered to be replaced by a plainer fly-fronted tunic (Bluse) in 1915, but they, together with the Waffenrock with some of the coloured piping and buttons removed, were all to be seen often in the same unit, until the end of the war.

Above: The 'Folks back home' thrilled at the idea of the glorious Cavalry charge to victory, and eagerly purchased postcards like the one above. In fact, after 1914 the cavalry rarely got the chance to charge anywhere. Left: German infantryman 1914, dressed in the 1910 field uniform. Around his neck hangs extra ammunition in a cloth bandolier. Below: While the Flower of Germany's youth marched off to war the older and less healthy joined the Reserve, to do guard and escort duty, and police work. The Germans too could laugh at themselves.

30

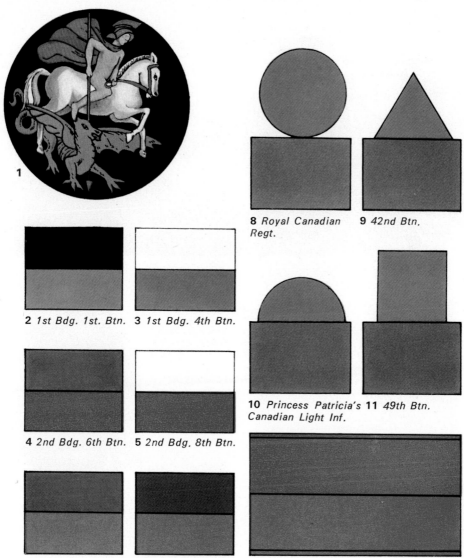

8 *Royal Canadian*   **9** *42nd Btn.*
Regt.

2 *1st Bdg. 1st. Btn.*   **3** *1st Bdg. 4th Btn.*

4 *2nd Bdg. 6th Btn.*   **5** *2nd Bdg. 8th Btn.*

10 *Princess Patricia's* **11** *49th Btn.*
Canadian Light Inf.

6 *3rd Bdg. 10th Btn.* **7** *3rd Bdg. 11th Btn.*   **12** *Armband: British Expeditionary Force.*

1 *St. George, patron saint of the cavalryman, was the Cavalry Corps badge on the Western Front from October 1914 to March 1919.* **2** *to* **7** *Cloth arm patches of the 1st Australian division which served on the Western Front 1916-1918.* **8** *to* **11** *Cloth arm patches belonging to the 3rd Canadian Division 7th Infantry Brigade in France for most of the war.* **12** *Coloured arm bands were worn by staff officers— this one indicates the General Headquarters of the British Expeditionary Force.*

German Hussars wore their distinctive Hussar dress, very colourful in full dress uniform, in field-grey for campaign. Their fur caps were covered with cloth. All cavalrymen carried light tubular steel lances. Toward the end of the war most of them served on foot in the trenches. Right: Hussar's attila braided tunic in field-grey (Marcus Hinton).

European royalty supplied many German regiments with honorary colonels. Soldiers wore their monograms on the shoulder-strap, instead of the usual regimental number (Artists collection).

The Germans, too, thought God was on their side. This belt plate, worn by all Prussian troops, bears the motto 'Gott Mit Uns'—God with Us (Artists collection).

German artillerymen haul their 77 mm field gun through the ever-present mud.

The War Lords. Field-Marshal Paul von Hindenburg 1847-1934 and General Erich Ludendorff 1865-1937. Both wear the leather Pickelhaube helmet. The spikes were longer for officers. (Rank and file removed theirs before going into action.) The cloth cover was worn on campaign, officers' helmets often being expensively made, with gilded metal and enamelled badges. Generals wore a double red stripe down their trouser-legs.

The Eagle of Prussia, worn on the front of the leather Pickelhaube (Artists collection).

33

Belgian Lancers, 1914. The gallant Belgian army fought back with a ferocity that shook the Germans. Almost destroyed, its gay uniforms gone forever, the Belgian army was reorganized and fought on, khaki clad.

THE BELGIAN ARMY

It was the Belgian army which received the first shock of the German attack in 1914. The little country was caught in the middle of reorganising her military defences. She could field only six infantry divisions and one of cavalry, a total of perhaps 200,000 men (and there were no reservists to call upon, as compulsory military service had only been introduced a year earlier). Both training and equipment were to prove inadequate. The mainstay of the Belgian infantry was the 7.65 mm Mauser M1889 rifle, but ammunition was in such short supply that range practice is said to have been restricted to one bullet per man per week. Machine-guns were also scarce. It was a time of change, and although field uniforms were being considered, it was not until 1915 that materials and styles dating from the 1850s were finally replaced by khaki on the British pattern for the whole army. About the same time steel helmets of the French type and brown leather equipment were also adopted.

THE AMERICAN ARMY

The entry of the USA into the war in April, 1917 meant that huge additional resources became available to the Allied cause—but not immediately. There was virtually no American army and men had to be conscripted and then trained. They had little equipment and few weapons. Tanks, guns, helmets, horses and even rifles had to be supplied by the British and French. Nevertheless, the first American contingent arrived in Paris in June, 1917. By the end of the war the US had 2,000,000 men in France and 4,000,000 under arms.

Both officers and men wore the 'olive-drab' field and service uniform that had been introduced in 1902, but the large quantities of this material required to fit out the American forces meant that the colour varied from a mustard green to brown. The officers favoured high brown boots, while most of the men wore puttees. The officers exhibited their marks of rank on their shoulder straps and the rankers wore a bronze US disc as their right-hand collar badge, and the appropriate branch badge on the left. The Springfield M1903 was the prescribed rifle of the infantry, but was in short supply so the Winchester and Remington production lines, which were already turning out Enfield designed rifles for the British army, adapted the weapons to take the American cartridge. The result was the P.17, a reliable but heavy model. Additional items adopted when the American forces reached Europe included British type steel helmets, brown leather Sam Browne belts and gas masks.

Adaptations also had to be made to the way in which the American soldier carried his equipment. Initially, he sported a 'long pack', which was a badly designed set of kit extending from head height down the back to below the waist. This meant, that without first removing the pack, sitting down was almost impossible and if one attempted to lie down the helmet was tipped over the eyes.

British soldiers, wearing tin hats or peaked caps, share the news that the war is over with their American allies. The US soldiers wear their overseas soft cap or the British designed helmet. The infantryman on the left wears the 1902 webbing equipment and the badly designed and uncomfortable 'long pack' (Imperial War Museum).

The War Years

1914   **June:** Franz Ferdinand assassinated at Sarajevo. **July:** Austro-Hungary declares war on Serbia. **August:** General outbreak of World War I (see page 5). Germany invades Belgium. Germany invades Poland. Russia invades East Prussia. Battle of Tannenburg, on the Eastern Front. Battle of Mons on Western Front. **September:** 1st Battle of the Marne. **October:** 1st Battle of Warsaw. 1st Battle of Ypres. **December:** 2nd Battle of Warsaw. Western Front stabilises. German cruiser force shells the English East Coast. Christmas truce on the Western Front.

1915   **January:** French offensive on the Western Front. **February:** The British Navy attack the Dardanelles. **March:** Battle of Neuve Chapelle. **April:** 2nd Battle of Ypres. ANZAC landings at Gallipoli. Death of poet Rupert Brooke at Scyros. **April to August:** Russians driven out of Poland at a cost of 750,000 prisoners. **May:** Italy joins Allies. Lusitania sunk. 2nd French offensive on the Western Front. In Britain, 157 people are killed in a railway crash at Gretna Green. **June:** 1st Charlie Chaplin film showing in London. **September:** Battle of Loos. **October:** The Central Powers overrun Serbia. **December:** The Allies evacuate the Gallipoli peninsula. Haig replaces Sir John French as the C-in-C of British forces.

1916   **January:** Military conscription introduced in Britain. **February to July:** Battle of Verdun. **Easter Week:** Sinn Fein rebellion in Dublin, fighting for Irish independence. **May:** Naval Battle of Jutland. **June:** British Minister of War, Lord Kitchener, is drowned in HMS Hampshire. Russians attack Poland and lose one million casualties. **July to November:** 1st Battle of the Somme. **August:** Rumania joins the Allies. **September:** Tanks are used in battle for the first time by the British. Lt Leefe Robinson, RFC, shoots down a Zeppelin near Enfield and is awarded the Victoria Cross. **November:** Death of Emperor Franz Joseph of Austria. **December:** Lloyd George becomes Prime Minister of Britain.

1917   **January:** Turks are driven from Egypt. **February:** Germany renews unlimited submarine warfare on Allied shipping. **March:** Germany retreats to the Hindenberg line on the Western Front. Abdication of Czar Nicholas II. **March to November:** Russian revolutions. **April:** USA declares war on the Central Powers. **April to December:** French offensive on the Western Front. **June:** Battle of Messines. **July:** Greece joins the Allies. **August to November:** 3rd Battle of Ypres, including Passchendaele. **December:** Armistice between Russia and the Central Powers agreed. Turks driven from Palestine.

1918   **March:** German offensive on the Western Front. Treaty of Brest-Litovsk signed between Germany and Russia. **April:** Marshal Foch is appointed supreme Allied commander. **July:** 2nd Battle of the Marne. Czar Nicholas and his family are murdered. **August to November:** Allied breakthrough on the Western Front. **September:** Armistice is signed between Bulgaria and the Allies. **October:** Armistice is signed between Turkey and the Allies. German fleet mutinies. **November:** Armistice is signed between Austria and the Allies. Poet Wilfred Owen is killed. Germany signs armistice with Allies.

1914

THE PATTERN IS ESTABLISHED

In the years before the outbreak of war the General Staff officers of both Germany and France had worked out their plans of campaign in readiness for war whenever it might come.

The German war plan had been devised by Count Schlieffen but he was now dead and its execution was entrusted to von Moltke. The idea was to break French resistance before Russian mobilisation made the danger of a war on two fronts serious. German troops were to wheel in a great arc through Belgium and north-eastern France thus outflanking the French fortifications system and fall upon Paris. The weight of the attack was to be on the right flank alongside the Channel coast, while the left was comparatively lightly held against the expected French counter-attack of Plan 17, that is, into Germany through the former French departments of Alsace and Lorraine.

Consequently, at 8.40 am on Tuesday, August 4, 1914 German cavalry spearheaded the invasion of Belgium in a lightning bid to seize the bridges over the River Meuse. Britain transferred a small but well-equipped expeditionary force to France but Belgium was soon overrun and the British and French armies were driven back. Sir John French, leading the British, was forced to retreat from the battlefields of Mons in a north-easterly direction. But this 'contemptible' little army, as the Kaiser called it, delayed the Germans, and, as events turned out, thereby helped to save Paris. The Germans then turned towards the south and almost cut off the French armies from their capital. General Joffre launched a flank attack from Paris and the reorganised British were ordered to strengthen the French line. After a desperate battle the Germans were driven back from the River Marne. Next they tried to break through to the Channel ports, but again they failed.

A pattern had been set. For the next four years the war on the Western Front was mainly fought by two lines of men, hidden underground in trenches, and hurling high explosives, poison gas and bullets at one another, often from a range of many miles. Thousands were to be smashed by shells, shot, burned and gassed. Wounded were to hang for days on the barbed wire between the lines until they died. Hundreds of thousands were to be mown down in a series of murderous offensives which seldom achieved anything.

Surprisingly, in 1899, a Polish banker had anticipated just such a stalemate when he said, 'Everybody will be entrenched in the next war. It will be a great war of entrenchment. The spade will be as indispensible to the soldier as his rifle'.

Unhesitatingly, from all parts of the British Empire, Australians, Canadians, Indians, New Zealanders, Rhodesians and South Africans came to adopt Britain's cause as their own, and to fight side by side in the trenches. This demonstration of brotherhood and unity in Britain's hour of need was one civilised and worthwhile episode in the sordid war story. The photograph shows a Canadian infantry Battalion (Imperial War Museum).

'I adore war. It is like a big picnic without the objectlessness of a picnic. I have never been so well or so happy.' (Captain the Hon J. H. F. Grenfell, DSO, 1st Royal Dragoons.) A lull in the fighting during the Battle of Festubert allows officers in reserve to enjoy a civilised meal (Imperial War Museum).

In the first few months of the war—French cavalry (left) in 1914, in uniforms little changed since the Crimean War, pass British artillery.

That truce! Christmas Eve, 1914. At several places along the Western Front the allied soldiers saw lights twinkling in the German trenches, then came the sound of singing. Finally came the enemy himself, waving lanterns and singing carols. The British and French put down their rifles and rose from their frozen burrows to greet their unexpected guests. Hands were shaken and gifts exchanged. A Christian peace reigned over the battlefield for a few precious hours, but never again would the killing be interrupted for such trivialities (Imperial War Museum).

Field Marshal Sir John French, Commander in Chief of the British expeditionary force— highly-trained, efficient troops, virtually wiped out in the first Battle of Ypres. Unpopular in certain Government circles, at the end of 1915 he was replaced by Haig (Imperial War Museum).

'That's us with him just before he went to France. The last time we saw him, poor fellow.'

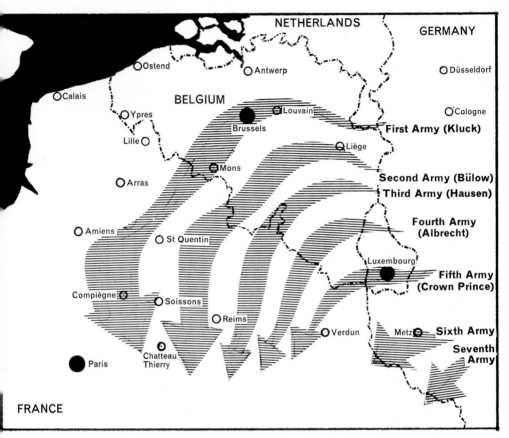

NETHERLANDS
GERMANY

○ Ostend
○ Antwerp
○ Düsseldorf

BELGIUM
○ Ypres
● Brussels
● Louvain
○'Cologne
First Army (Kluck)
Lille ○
○ Liège

○ Arras
● Mons
Second Army (Bülow)
Third Army (Hausen)

○ Amiens
○ St Quentin
Fourth Army (Albrecht)

Luxembourg
Fifth Army (Crown Prince)
Compiègne ○
○ Soissons

○ Reims
○ Verdun
Metz ○ **Sixth Army**
Seventh Army

● Paris
Chatteau Thierry

○ Calais

FRANCE

The original Von Schlieffen Plan called for the German armies to sweep through Belgium and France to encircle Paris. However the plan was changed and five German armies cut a swathe through the Allied defences along the frontier in August 1914. Exhausted, the Germans were driven back from the Marne and the war settled down along a line that hardly changed during the next four years.

During September 1914, the following question was posed in an edition of the London Evening News, 'Would it not be wonderful if the English Bowmen (presumably of Crecy fame), led by Saint George appeared to aid the small British Army at Mons!' In early 1915 troops on the Western Front who had heard of the article began to circulate the story and rumours spread rapidly. Apparently, the rumours even reached the enemy trenches and tales were told of knights in shining armour riding into battle accompanied by angelic hosts. Thus it was that the famous story of the angels at Mons was born.

1915

THE ALLIES WITH THEIR BACKS TO THE WALL

The year of 1915 was not a good one for the Allies. Italy, after promises of Austrian territory had joined them, but Bulgaria had decided to join the Central Powers and soon overran Serbia.

On the Western Front little changed. Despite the use of poison gas the Germans were unable to break the British line at Ypres, and the British only gained a few yards of ground as a result of attacks at Neuve Chapelle in March and the Battle of Loos in September. This was also the year when Sir Douglas Haig replaced Sir John French as commander of the British forces.

In May, 1915 the ocean liner *Lusitania* was sunk by German vessels off the Irish coast and over 100 neutral American citizens perished. This wholly unjustified act caused hysterical outbursts from the Allied populations and led to increasing bitterness between the fighting troops.

In the same year an attempt was made to break through Turkish territory to Russia and an Allied assault was made on the Dardanelles. Unfortunately, all hope of surprise was lost by an unsuccessful naval attack in February-March. So when a combined attack of troops and ships was made in the next month, the Turkish defenders were ready, and in spite of great heroism the attempt had to be abandoned at the end of the year. The armies of the Central Powers were therefore free to overrun the Balkans, leaving only Salonika in Allied hands.

A burial party (right). Initially horrific, such work was soon to become part of everyday routine. In a little over four years 1,000,000 British servicemen died.

German troops digging in, Argonne, November 1915. 'The familiar trench smell of 1915-17 still haunts my nostrils', wrote Robert Graves, 'compounded of stagnant mud, latrine buckets, chloride of lime, unburied or half-buried corpses, rotting sandbags, stale human sweat, fumes of cordite and lyddite' (Imperial War Museum).

Count Bernstorff, German ambassador in Washington until early 1917, warned Americans against sailing in the Lusitania (Imperial War Museum).

Seeing which way the wind was blowing, Italy elected to join the Allies and in May, 1915 declared war on Austria-Hungary. Their King is seen here at the Italian Front (Imperial War Museum).

Visitors to the Front. Major Winston Churchill, wearing a French shrapnel helmet, poses with General Fayolle (Imperial War Museum).

The Flame-Thrower. This terrible weapon had a range of about 50 yards. First used by the Germans in 1915 and the British in 1916 (Imperial War Museum).

Even horses had to learn gas-mask drill. The Germans lost the advantage of a surprise attack by trying it out on a small scale first. (Just as the British prematurely introduced their tank to the enemy) (Imperial War Museum).

British and French soldiers relax. They now wear steel helmets during leisure periods as well as in the trenches. First issued to British troops in 1915, there were only enough for the men in the front line, who handed them over on being relieved. Experiments were also made with body armour. The Italians, for example, supplied it to personnel detailed to leave their trenches under the cover of darkness, and to attempt to cut paths through the barbed wire protecting the enemy lines.

1916

THE YEAR OF LOST OPPORTUNITIES

Sir Douglas Haig had now succeeded Sir John French as Commander in Chief in France. Steel helmets were becoming more familiar than the smarter but softer peaked cap. In 1916 also, for the first time in British history it became necessary to introduce conscription. A result of this move was a tremendous Allied attack on the Western Front. The British gained some success along the River Somme but only after very heavy losses and with the assistance of the tank, an enclosed armoured vehicle with caterpillar wheels, which, if greater numbers had been available at this time, might have proved a decisive factor in the mud and barbed wire of northern France. Nevertheless, the German line held, and further south they attempted to advance at Verdun. This was a tactical move designed to break the deadlock and maybe bleed France to death. The area around Verdun was not of great military importance. Indeed, much of its artillery had been moved to defend more valuable positions. Falken-hayn, the German general responsible for the attack, knew, however, that for historical and patriotic reasons the French would not yield the area without a bitter sacrifice of men and munitions. The result was a terrible battle in which over 400,000 Frenchmen were killed. But in spite of German pressure Verdun held out and its defence is one of the great French exploits of the war.

At sea British power had not yet been challenged, but in May, 1916 the German warships made a dash out of Kiel Harbour. They were met by the British Fleet under Admiral Jellicoe off the coast of Denmark at the Battle of Jutland. Both sides recorded hits in the fog which enveloped the two fleets for much of the engagement, but when British reinforcements arrived the Germans retreated to the safety of their harbours and remained there until the end of the war two years later.

But in 1916 too, the German submarines or 'U' boats began to sink all ships trading with the Allied countries, and soon were destroying many thousands of tons of shipping a week. This caused shortages in Britain and food had to be rationed. Everyone was issued with a ration card to make sure that the supplies of foodstuffs which did reach British shores were fairly distributed. Defeat of the Allied nations was very near. The next year, however, saw the introduction of the convoy system and the development of camouflage and depth-charges which protected merchant shipping.

Such patriotic pictures (right) were entitled: 'To the last Frenchman', 'Into the jaws of Hell', and 'France's crucifixion'.

Administrators of the Allied war machine, August 1916: General Joffre, French Premier Poincaré, George V, General Foch and General Haig (Imperial War Museum).

Lloyd George sees for himself. The Prime Minister was well aware that the horrors of the fighting at the Front were frequently kept from him, and he opposed what he considered to be the often wasteful tactics of his general (Imperial War Museum).

The British surprise weapon of the Somme recalls with its inscription the fated Cunard liner. The message is clear: 'Remember what you did to the Lusitania as you run before me'.

Germany declared war on Portugal, Britain's oldest ally, in March, 1916. Seemingly well-nourished Portuguese troops help themselves to their daily food rations (Imperial War Museum).

Two British soldiers snatch their dinner rations in the vicinity of the Somme, October, 1916. Allied losses were to reach 600,000 before the battle for the Somme was over (Imperial War Museum).

A routine foot inspection for the men of the 12th East Yorkshires. The feet of many men literally rotted in the rain-filled trenches (Imperial War Museum).

Cleaning up, sporting a trophy of the war on his head. Men of the 1st Anzac Division relaxing after taking Pozieres, July, 1916 (Imperial War Museum).

Two Frenchmen at the battle for Verdun. Not of great military importance, Verdun was historically important to the French. Falkenhayn, recognising this, hoped to bleed France dry in one concentrated effort. 'Humanity . . . must be mad to do what it is doing. What scenes of horror and carnage. . . . Hell cannot be so terrible.'

King George V decorating Marshal Petain, hero at Verdun. Twenty-four years later Petain signed an armistice with Germany and set up a quasi-independent administration at Vichy.

For him the war is over. A German prisoner of war in 1916 wearing his original field-grey uniform with piping and buttons (Imperial War Museum).

1917

THE YEAR THE TIDE TURNED

1917 was the turning point of the war. The situation for the Allies improved.

On March 17 the Czar of Russia, Nicholas II, abdicated partly as a result of his armies being defeated by the Germans and Austrians. Alexander Kerensky became head of the Russian Government and remained loyal to the Allies for a time, but he was replaced by Lenin, who, on December 15, made peace with the Germans. Russia was thus out of the war and Britain had lost an ally.

However, American shipping had been attacked by the Germans and so, in April, the United States of America declared war on Germany. In consequence of this, the Germans prepared to make a supreme effort to overrun the Allies before American men and supplies could reach the battlelines. Battles raged in France at Vimy, Messines and Passchendale and the Central Powers made a determined effort to drive Italy out of the war, as they had done with Russia and the Balkan States. British and French troops were sent to strengthen the Italians and the situation was saved.

Elsewhere the Allies were more successful. General Allenby marched from Egypt, defeated the Turks, and on Christmas Day, Jerusalem was in the hands of Christian soldiers. The dream of King Richard the Lion Hearted and the Crusaders thus came true after seven hundred years. The British who had been in Mesopotamia (Iraq), were now able to take the offensive and General Maude recaptured Kut.

The United States enters the war (overleaf), and not before time, thought many people in Britain. But a majority of Americans thought otherwise. Why should they become involved in Europe's quarrels? Many tons of neutral American shipping was attacked and damaged before Germany's unrestricted 'U' Boat action forced President Wilton to declare war (Imperial War Museum).

51

Typical of the war along the Western Front. The mud, the craters and the misery of Passchendaele in 1917 (Imperial War Museum).

'When you can advance no more, dig in and hold on', was the military motto of both sides. The wire stretched over this German trench was intended to prevent enemy infantry from jumping in (Imperial War Museum).

The rain has turned to snow and the mud is frozen. It is February, 1917 and in the worst winter since 1880-81 the British prepare to attack at Arras.

Like so many British commanders, Field Marshal, Viscount Allenby first won a reputation as a cavalry leader. As the Germans pressed forward in the dark, opening days of the war, he was conspicuous at Mons. In the subsequent withdrawal of British troops he led a cavalry division with great skill. By 1917 he was an army commander (3rd Army), and again distinguished himself at the Battle of Arras. It was in the Middle East, however that Allenby's most decisive achievements were to take place. In 1917 he captured Gaza, through positive and inspired leadership. Jerusalem was freed from Turkish rule just before Christmas and his successes helped to relieve the Allies' gloom over the stalemate on the Western Front. Allenby's task in the last months of the war was the final defeat of the Turkish army. His troops won decisive victories in the Battles of Megiddo (Sept. and Oct. 1918) and then advanced beyond the Jordan valley to Damascus and Aleppo. With the arrival of peace, a grateful country promoted him Field Marshal, made him a Viscount and awarded him £50,000.

General Sir Edmund Allenby, who made the dreams of the old Crusaders come true when he led a Christian army into Jerusalem in December, 1917 (Imperial War Museum).

Those London 'buses came in useful'. It is quite well known that they were converted into troop carriers like these being utilised after heavy fighting at Monchy le Preux in April, 1917. But they were also found to be ideal as mobile pigeon lofts. In the absence of radio communication, the birds were used extensively for getting messages from the Front back to Head Quarters (Imperial War Museum).

1918

ONE LAST BIG EFFORT

As Russia had withdrawn from the war it was possible by the spring of 1918 for Germany to move troops and supplies from her eastern borders and to concentrate her energies upon the Western Front. This last big effort of the Central Powers was known as the 'Michael' offensive.

The attack pushed the Allied line back to within twenty miles of Amiens, and in places almost broke through. But General Foch was made supreme commander of the Allied armies, and fresh, well-equipped American troops were now beginning to reach Europe in large numbers. Soon the Allies were able to counterattack. Serbia was liberated. Bulgaria surrendered and Turkey sued for peace. The old Austrian Empire finally broke up under Italian pressure and the last of Germany's partners was disposed of in the late summer.

The Germans themselves were steadily driven back in France. Their nation was losing heart. They were being partially starved by the Allied blockade of many Channel and North Sea ports. Their navy was in a state of mutiny. Discontent with their government was growing and revolts were breaking out in Berlin and other major cities. Groups of Freikorps were trying to crush the elements of unrest, but finally their Emperor abdicated and fled to neutral Holland.

The Great War 'to end all wars' was over. Millions of pounds had been spent and probably nine million lives lost yet every country was in a worse state after the war than before it.

In the Spring of 1918 the Germans began to withdraw to the Hindenburg Line and as they retreated they systematically destroyed all that remained of the already devastated countryside. (Overleaf) buildings were looted and set on fire, entire villages were smashed to the ground, cemeteries were desecrated and whole orchards cut down.
Such photographs brought home to countrymen and farmers the world over the waste that war could inflict on a lifetime of work (Imperial War Museum).

The General Staff in 1918. Haig and some of his Army commanders who were often criticised as being divorced from the brutal facts of life at the Front (Imperial War Museum).

Foch, the 'Man of Orleans', appointed by the Allied armies to co-ordinate the action on the Western Front. An appointment long overdue (Imperial War Museum).

French cavalry, still armed with lances, passes through a village near Neulette. They had waited in reserve to be used once the breakthrough promised by Plan 17 materialised. They were still waiting in 1918 (Imperial War Museum).

Guns as well as manpower did their part in halting the final German offensives of 1918. Later in the year they were moved up as the Allies returned to the attack. These are 18 pounders crossing the Canal du Nord in September. There are only four horses to each team instead of the customary six because at this time many British animals were on loan to the American army (Imperial War Museum).

The battle for Amiens has been lost, but are these German prisoners despondent that, for them, the war is over?

British prisoners taken in the battles in front of Bapaume being fed from a German field kitchen. Both sides used photographs of prisoners for propaganda purposes. The elderly, smallest or sickly always in the foreground to emphasise the difficulties that the enemy was having in raising recruits (Imperial War Museum).

The old men, the women, the children and what remains of Lille welcome the 57th Division of the Liverpool Irish with the end of the war in sight. October, 1918 (Imperial War Museum).

'Pack up your troubles in your old kit bag, and smile, smile, smile.' They can afford to smile. The war has been raging for four years now and they are still alive. Four months more and they can pack up and go home.

'Wipers' to the British. To the Belgians, Ypres, population 20,000, situated on the River Yperlee south-west of Bruges and important for lace and linen manufactures. The photograph shows a scene typical of the old town after four years of shelling, bombing, attack and counter-attack (Imperial War Museum).

1919

THE AFTERMATH

In Germany a Republic was declared and its leaders immediately sent envoys to the Allied lines. Early in the morning of November 8, 1918, Erzberger, the leading representative of the German Government, arrived at the temporary headquarters in the forest of Compiegne of Marshal Foch, the supreme Allied Commander. Apparently, the German delegation at first requested Foch's proposals for a possible armistice so that they might be considered by the German command. Foch, however, gave the impression that his country was not prepared to make any such proposals, but would, in all probability, continue the conflict. The Germans were therefore forced into the humiliating position of asking, almost begging, for an armistice.

The terms of the armistice were going to be harsh. Germany was to be severely punished for her mistakes. Already the Kaiser had abdicated and fled from his country leaving it in the throes of famine and revolution and now mutiny and disorder were spreading throughout the German speaking world.

By the subsequent Treaty of Versailles Germany was compelled to admit responsibility for the war and measures of punishment followed as a matter of course. She was disarmed and had to surrender her ships, large guns and tanks. Her army and navy were drastically reduced and her air force abolished. The region of Alsace and Lorraine was returned to France and some outlying areas on Germany's borders were allowed to detach themselves and join neighbouring countries instead. All former German colonies were now to be administered by other nations. The left bank of the River Rhine was to be patrolled by the Allies for a further fifteen years and during this period the French were to work the valuable coal mines of the Saar region. Finally, Germany was expected to pay £100,000,000 a year for sixty-six years as compensation for her war crimes.

A war so vast was bound to bring about equally large changes. World trade had been dislocated and much industry destroyed so that previously wealthy countries now found themselves poor. Belgium and north-east France were left in ruins, orchards and fields laid waste, factories and mines destroyed. Russia was suffering from poverty and revolution. The Britain of George V which had been the most powerful country in the world, survived, but was shaken, and had now been overtaken by the United States of America as an industrial and maritime power. Yet these nations had been the victors on the battlefields.

The National Debts of the Allied countries had risen to figures which only a professor of mathematics could hope to understand. Neither Tommy, the Poilus nor the Doughboys returned home to lands fit for heroes. Many felt let down by the Establishment and depression, unemployment and violence were much in evidence in the wasted years following 1918.

Europe itself was changed. The map showed new countries where great empires had existed before. Families which had ruled for centuries, such as the Hapsburgs in Austria-Hungary and the Romanoffs in Russia lost their thrones. Many who had signed-up as teenagers in 1914 now found themselves restless, untrained and unsuited to civilian life. (There were those ex-service men who would automatically drop to the ground and cover their heads if a car back-fired).

But from the bewildered, faceless crowds new men were to emerge. In Russia a magnetic orator called Lenin; in Germany, in the trappings of an air-ace, Hermann Goering, later to be commander of the German air force in another tragic war; in France a tiger named Clemenceau: Britain discovered the dynamic personalities of Lloyd George and Winston Churchill, and in General Pershing the United States of America had her first modern war hero. But most significant of all were to be the violent political beliefs of an Austrian corporal in a Bavarian infantry regiment, Adolf Hitler.

For over four years Europe had fought the greatest war in its long history, yet in 1918 the continent remained seething with fear, hate and suspicion. The seeds of future discord only lay dormant. How ironic that 'the war to end all wars' has become known as 'the First World War'.

THE WESTERN FRONT 1914-18

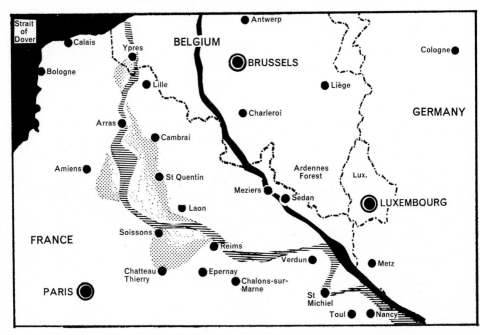

The dotted area represents the extreme advances of both sides. The horizontally lined area shows the Western Front for most of the war (1914-17). The darker line shows the Armistice line of 1918.

Two faces in the crowd looking into the future, waiting their call. Winston Churchill and Bernard Montgomery watching a march past in Lille only a month before hostilities ceased (Imperial War Museum).

The Tools of War

All the armies experimented with armour. The weight of it was the main problem, so it was usually worn only by special assault units or more static but exposed snipers and machine-gunners. The picture shows Irish Guardsmen with captured German body armour and an armoured machine gun (Imperial War Museum).

Helmets. Top, from left to right: British, Belgian 1917 with visor; middle: Portuguese, Franco-American 1917 Dunand with visor, German sniper's protective mask (weight 14½ lb); bottom: German with extra-heavy plate on the front, Austrian. Each nation developed its own style or type of helmet, but many followed the basic French design: a small bowl fitting like a skull-cap. By 1915 it had a raised central crest and was decorated on the front with a bursting grenade. The familiar German helmet, more practical and comfortable than the British steel helmet, and stronger than the French, was first issued in 1916 to the troops attempting to capture Verdun (Imperial War Museum).

First used by the Germans but soon adopted by the Allies, gas was to become a feared and horrible weapon. Soldiers wearing gas masks looked grotesque. Here are German prisoners bringing in their wounded (Imperial War Museum).

The humour of war—an inscribed, possibly looted, bell serving as a gas alarm in trenches near Beaumont Hamel (Imperial War Museum).

65

German artillery repair shop at Tourcoiny. Some German cannons were so worn after years of firing that the shells often failed to reach the Allied trenches, and fell instead on German infantrymen. Recoil buffers were introduced which allowed the barrel to recoil without moving the carriage, enabling it to resume its position almost immediately. These and better loading techniques improved the firing power of field guns at an incredible rate during the war.

The orchestra which provided the background music to life on The Western Front. Closest to the line were the field guns, further back would be the 60 pounders and 6 inch guns, then the 9.2 howitzers and far in the rear the 15 inch howitzers and 12 inch guns on railway mountings (Imperial War Museum).

The 'Big Berthas' produced by the Krupp factories of Essen, and used in both World Wars, were named after Frau Bertha von Bohlen, a proprietor of the organisation. They were of varied calibre, although usually 8.25 inches. The barrels were 126 feet long, and the total weight of the gun was 154 tons. Shells of up to 330 pounds could be fired. One of these guns shelled Paris in the Spring of 1918 from a distance of over 70 miles. On Good Friday a direct hit was scored on the church of St. Gervais and 88 people were killed, 68 others being injured.

Wire everywhere—if it is not barbed, it is telephone. Here artillery officers north-east of Arras in April 1917 are observing fire and sending back the results to their gunners (Imperial War Museum).

Machine-gun bay in the Allied front line. Over 240,500 machine-guns were manufactured in Britain during the war. It was so feared and hated by the enemy that machine-gunners could expect no quarter when at the mercy of attacking troops.

A less violent attempt to win over the enemy. Men of the Hampshire Regiment releasing propaganda balloons near Bethune in September, 1918 (Imperial War Museum).

Loading shells for the 'war of attrition'. 'We have a larger population than them, so if we continue to kill one another off at approximately the same rate, there will come a time when they run out of men before us.' Note the railway track. Before the outbreak of hostilities the German policy had been to build not fortresses but lines of communication. As the war developed, light railways were laid right up to the Front (Imperial War Museum).

As wireless was not perfected, communication between units along the Front was often difficult. A system of signalling with rockets was developed, but single shots were almost impossible to recognise in the heat of a bombardment. After dark, their varieties of colour gave an air of festivity to the night. Those illustrated here are SOS rockets belonging to the Sixth Battalion York and Lancaster Regiment (Imperial War Museum).

'The spade will be as indispensable to the soldier as his rifle', wrote a far-seeing Polish banker in 1899.
A British wiring party is carrying corkscrew supports between Arras and Fenchy in the late Spring of 1917. The construction of obstacles to thwart the enemy's advances was a laborious, but skilled and important task. Many hundred thousand miles of barbed wire must have been used along the Western Front. Wooden pallisades were used in medieval battles for this purpose (Imperial War Museum).

The Agony of War

The victims of war, May 1918. Retiring French troops accompany refugees made homeless after heavy fighting along the River Aisne (Imperial War Museum).

The Victim. Caught up in the slaughter. He didn't want to fight anyway.

The Veteran. He's seen it all and lived to tell the tale.

The improvisations of war, March 1918. Walking British wounded use old prams to move stretcher cases after heavy fighting along the River Somme (Imperial War Museum).

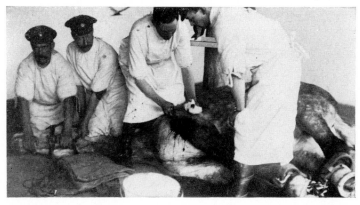

An innocent sufferer of the war is held down while shrapnel is removed from his tortured body (Imperial War Museum).

71

The ever-present horrors of the battlefield led many to doubt their beliefs, while to others their faith was their only comfort. Each fighting nation believed that God was on its side, which led J. C. Squire to write:
God heard the embattled nations sing and shout
Gott strafe England—God save the King—
God this—God that—and God the other thing.
My God, said God, I've got my work cut out (Imperial War Museum).

Sisters in the Order of St. John of Jerusalem (Imperial War Museum).

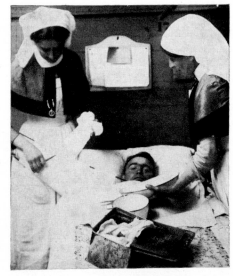

Comfortable sight to the wounded—Red Cross nurses. Sisters bandaging another victim on board their medical barge near Aisne in the Spring of 1918 (Imperial War Museum).

The results of war—patients at Roehampton are taught to use their artificial limbs (Imperial War Museum).

The comradeship of war. Fellow sufferers: British wounded and German prisoner.

Dead soldiers of the Fatherland lie in the soil of the country which they came to conquer —5,000 German graves at Sailly sur la Lys (Imperial War Museum).

Glossary...
An ABC of Terms
from the Great War

ANZAC These initials refer to the Australian and New Zealand Army Corps who distinguished themselves during the Gallipoli assault in 1915.

BEF The British Expeditionary Force: a small but highly trained British army which fought in France in 1914 and was almost wiped out at the first Battle of Ypres.

Black Hand This was a secret society which attempted to promote a single Slav state in south-east Europe. Gavrilo Princip, the Serbian student who assassinated Franz Ferdinand at Sarajevo, was a member.

Blitzkrieg This means a lightning war, and was the description used by the Germans for a fast and violent campaign that would smash all opposition.

Casualties On 24 August, 1914, 353 men of the 4th Middlesex regular battalion were killed or wounded along the canal bank by Nimy Bridge and in positions southwards at Mons. They were the first British soldiers to fall in battle in northern Europe for 99 years. Between 1 July and 18 November, 1916 the battle along the banks of the River Somme probably resulted in more deaths and casualties than any other theatre of war. Allied losses were over 600,000, many of them young volunteers, 'the flower of Britain's youth'. 18,000 are said to have died in one day.

Cornwall VC The Battle of Jutland was the first and only action of Boy First Class Cornwall. Only 17 years old he was the sight-setter for the crew manning the forward six-inch gun of *HMS Chester*. On his head he wore a set of earphones through which his instructions crackled from the gunnery officer. In front of him there was a brass wheel which he had to turn in order to raise or lower the muzzle of his gun. In the late afternoon of May 31st Admiral Hood ordered *HMS Chester* into the heart of the battle to assist Admiral Beatty's squadron which was already engaging the enemy. Before long Cornwall's gun was booming and recoiling as his ship came under fire from three or four German cruisers. The British vessel was in action for about twenty minutes only. The noise must have been head-splitting as tons of hot metal were hurled at her. The bitter fumes of cordite must have made John Cornwall's throat choke and his eyes weep; he was injured and faint with pain; the rest of his gun's crew were soon killed or severely wounded, but he remained at his post awaiting further orders. His devotion to duty was to cost him his young life, but it earned him the Victoria Cross, Britain's highest award for gallantry. He was buried with the full honours of the British Navy. A white ensign was used to cover his coffin and one of his wreaths was enscribed 'Faithful unto death'.

Dreadnought   This name for a class of battleship was derived from a vessel of nearly 18,000 tons and 500 feet in length which was launched at Portsmouth in 1906. It was revolutionary in that, by being powered by turbine engines, it made all existing warships obsolete. Germany soon copied the design and a race began to see which nation could build most ships.

Economy Committees   These were set up by large cities throughout Britain with the introduction of food rationing in 1916. Waste campaigns were also started. For example, Portsmouth schools, in four weeks in 1917, collected three tons of paper, twenty-four thousand bottles, over seven tons of metal and fifteen hundredweights of rags.

Ersatz   An astounding range of substitute or ersatz products were offered by German science during the war to replace natural commodities no longer available. In East Africa, for example, von Lettow-Vorbeck, the German Commander, attempted to produce motor fuel from coconuts.

Flag Days   Even before the war it was becoming the custom for an artificial flower to be given as a form of receipt to those members of the public who contributed to charity collections. Such an effective and popular arrangement was soon made applicable to the larger appeals which the war necessitated. As a result many flag days were organised —the decoration worn being a flag of the Nation for which the appeal was being made. The number and variety of these appeals were considerable and the public's response to them heart-warming. In Portsmouth, for example, there were twenty-three flag days between 1914 and 1918, and the total sum collected amounted to nearly £18,000.

Here are some of the charities for which collections were made:

Our Day (Red Cross)	Lifeboat Day	Italian Flag Day
Belgian Flag Day	Prisoners of War	Russian Flag Day
French Flag Day	Trafalgar Day	Serbian Flag Day

Foch, Ferdinand   This French general, sometimes known as 'the man of Orleans', in his late sixties became Supreme Allied Commander in March, 1918, and subsequently received the German surrender.

George V   This British king was a cousin to the German Kaiser and was also related to Nicholas II, the Czar of Russia. His grandfather had been Albert, the German prince who had married Queen Victoria. When Britain and Germany went to war George changed his German surname to Saxe-Coburg Gotha to Windsor.

Hari, Mata   Her real name was Gertrude Margarete Zel'le. She was a dancer on the French stage but became the epitome of the beautiful spy and one of the world's most infamous women. She was shot by the French in 1917.

Irony   It is an ironic fact that on the 4 August, 1914 the British and German fleets passed in full view of each other without a shot being fired. This came about because the two nations were not officially at war with each other until midnight by which time the British had dispersed to their battle stations, and the Germans had steamed for the safer waters of the Fatherland.

Jerry   This was a slang expression for a German, especially a German soldier. The British were known as Tommies, the French as Poilus and the Americans as Doughboys.

Kaiser   A title derived from the Latin Caesar and given to the emperors of the Old Holy Roman Empire, and of the rulers of the German Empire before the First World War. Wilhelm II was Kaiser from 1888 until his abdication in 1918. He died in the Netherlands in 1941.

Lusitania   A British Cunard liner launched in 1906 and remembered for her fateful voyage across the Atlantic Ocean in 1915, when she was sunk by a German submarine with a loss of over 1,300 lives. The action was one of the main causes of the eventual entry into the war of the United States of America.

Mascots   Some regiments took their pet animals with them on service. For example, the goat of the Royal Welch Fusiliers died during the retreat from Mons and was given a funeral with full military honours in a Belgian cemetery. Edinburgh Castle contains monuments to the various animals which helped and suffered with the Allies. Dogs, horses, reindeer, carrier pigeons, mice and canaries are all included.

No Man's Land   This was the ground between the two rows of opposing trenches, sometimes only yards apart, and where most of the casualties were suffered.

Nurses   Probably the most famous nurse of the First World War was Edith Cavell, a British woman serving in occupied Belgium. She was executed by the Germans on 12 October, 1915 for her role in aiding Allied wounded to escape to the Netherlands.

Orkney Islands   It was near these islands in the waters known as Scapa Flow that at 7.40 pm on 5 June, 1916 *HMS Hampshire* struck a German mine. The cruiser heeled over and sank in fifteen minutes carrying Lord Kitchener, the British Minister of War, to the bottom of the North Sea.

Poppies   Poppies are widespread throughout the world but they flourish in many of the areas traversed by the Western Front and sprang up in the shell-torn earth during the war. It is appropriate, therefore, that they should have been adopted as a remembrance emblem for those many servicemen who died in the wars against Germany: their colour reminding us of the blood that was shed for us.

Queen Elizabeth   In 1915 she was the prototype of Britain's latest battleship. Her eight 15-inch guns made her the most powerful vessel afloat, but she was badly damaged by shellfire and mines during the Gallipoli campaign.

Richthofen   Manfred von Richthofen, with approximately eighty victories to his credit, was Germany's most famous air-ace of the war. Another brilliant airman was Britain's Edward Mannock, who, despite being blind in one eye, claimed seventy-three kills.

Scrap of Paper   At the beginning of August, 1914 a long-standing treaty signed by the Great Powers guaranteed the neutrality of Belgium. Germany refused Britain's request to honour her pledge and invaded Belgium. She then complained that Britain declared war 'just for a scrap of paper'.

Spies   Quite early in the war a 'spy fever' swept through Britain and towns of special importance, like the south coast ports, were declared 'prohibited areas'. Austrian and German barbers, waiters and shop-keepers who, in some cases, had lived in Britain for many years, were interned, some in the Isle of Man, and other foreigners were expected to leave their districts. Despite such precautions, spies almost certainly remained at work in Britain's military and administrative centres. The enemy had in all probability infiltrated agents into the country well before the outbreak of hostilities, and it was easy enough for a German who spoke good English to pose as an Englishman and to make friends among servicemen and Government employees. His problem, however, was to get his information back to Germany. A variety of techniques came to light as the war progressed. Innocent-looking advertisements were sent to newspapers which would convey information to companion spies who had knowledge of a previously arranged code and who could get the information out of the country. Chess problems set in periodicals are also believed to have been used. Press editors were warned that they should make every effort to assure themselves of the nationality of their contributors and the legitimacy of their contributions.

Taxi Cab Army At one stage during the Battle of the Marne the Allies had to be reinforced by a brigade rushed out from Paris in taxicabs. This was probably the first tactical use of motorised infantry in a war that was full of innovations.

Truce On Christmas Day, 1914 firing stopped along much of the Western Front and British and German troops met in No Man's Land where they talked, exchanged cigarettes and chocolate, and, in some places, even organised football matches. But after a strong rebuke from their respective headquarters, the fighting resumed and those, who hours before had gossiped, again tried to kill each other.

U Boats Familiar abbreviation for *Unterseeboot* or the German submarine. They were extensively used against Allied shipping, and with considerable success, until counter-measures such as the convoy system, camouflage and depth-charges were developed.

Voie Sacrée This was a name given to the Verdun-Bar-le-Duc road along which Petain's defence of Verdun was supplied. Up to 3,500 lorries carried 4,000 tons of supplies and 15,000 to 20,000 men every day at the height of the siege. Nothing was allowed to interfere with the flow. All other vehicles were forbidden on the routeway; military transports which broke down were pushed aside, and the road surface was constantly repaired and renewed.

Women Without the sacrifices made by the women of Britain, and the way in which they took over traditionally male jobs, the war might not have been won. They became clerks in the business world, workers in munition factories, farm labourers and conductors on public transport. All this was undertaken in addition to their more usual role of housewife, mother and charity worker.

Yarmouth Together with the other east coast towns of Scarborough and Hartlepool, Yarmouth was suddenly bombarded by the German navy in November and December, 1914. These incidents really brought the war home to the British civilian population, stimulated recruitment to the army, and emphasised the important role which the British navy had in patrolling coastal waters.

Zeppelin A rigid balloon which could be steered was designed by Count von Zeppelin. It was used by the Germans for air raids on Britain, London being first bombed on 31 May, 1915.

Zimmermann Telegram This was a secret message sent by Zimmermann, the German Foreign Secretary, to the German ambassador in Mexico City, suggesting an alliance between the two countries and that

Mexico should regain control of Arizona, New Mexico and much of Texas if the United States of America should enter the war on the Allied side. The telegram was intercepted and decoded by British Intelligence and the information was passed to the American Government. The incident helped to bring American public support behind the Allies.

BOOKS FOR FURTHER READING

Non Fiction

Blunden, E. *Undertones of War*. Penguin, 1936. Autobiographical account of life at the Western Front.

Farrar-Hockley, A. *The Somme*. Pan, 1970. The tragedy and the terror of the fighting along the banks of this famous river.

Graves, R. *Goodbye to all That*. Penguin, 1969. Splendid, readable description of the author's experiences fighting in France.

Ribbons, I. *Tuesday, 4th August, 1914*. Oxford UP, 1970. An hour by hour account of the fateful first day of the war with examples drawn from many parts of the world.

Poetry

Up the Line to Death; The War Poets, 1914-1918. Edited by B. Gardner, Methuen, 1964. An anthology of poems by over seventy poets which illustrates the man at the Front's attitude as it declined from the exciting patriotism of 1914 to the bitter disillusionment of 1918.

Fiction

Barbusse, H. *Under Fire*. Published in 1916. General account of the early years of the war.

Hemingway, E. *A Farewell to Arms*. Penguin. Based upon the author's experiences when serving with the Italians during the war.

Remarque, E. M. *All Quiet on the Western Front*. Mayflower, 1968. Probably the best known war novel ever written. Describes the futility of war as seen through the eyes of an ordinary German soldier.

Other works of fiction which use the First World War and its aftermath as a background include:

Cronin, A. J. *The Citadel*
Greenwood, W. *Love on the Dole*
Isherwood, C. *Goodbye to Berlin*
Orwell, G. *Down and out in London and Paris*
Sheriff, R. C. *Journey's End*